The Little Boy Named Barry Obama

Children's Modern History

BABY PROFESSOR

EDUCATION KIDS

Speedy Publishing LLC
40 E. Main St. #1156
Newark, DE 19711
www.speedypublishing.com

Photos by Shutterstock.com, Evan El-Amin, David Peterlin,
Frederic Legrand - COMEO, Everett Collection, Drop of Light,
berlinpictures16, Ververidis Vasilis and Jose Gil

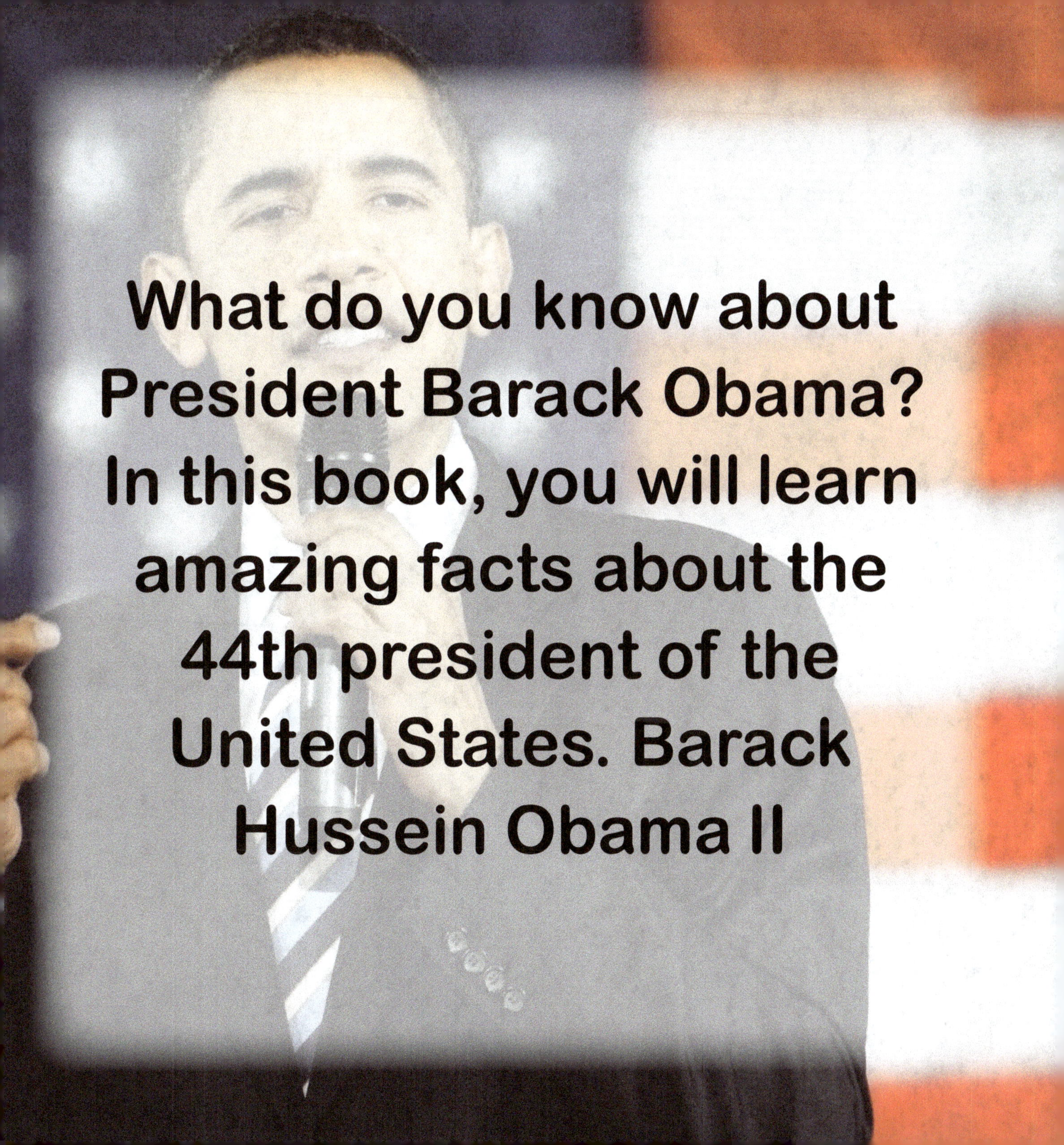

What do you know about President Barack Obama? In this book, you will learn amazing facts about the 44th president of the United States. Barack Hussein Obama II

He is the 44th President of the United States. Amazingly, the little boy, Barry Obama, became the first African American to become the leader of the United States.

He was born in Honolulu, Hawaii, which is outside the continental United States. He joined the world of politics in 1996. He served in the US Senate for three years.

Eventually, he joined the presidential election in 2008. He was recognized as a brilliant speaker. He spoke from the heart. His thoughts and ideas were brilliant. The once simple Barry Obama had become popular all over the world.

He was born on the 4th of August, 1961 in Honolulu, Hawaii. His parents are Ann Dunham from Kansas and Barack Obama, Sr. from Kenya.

But he grew up without his dad because his parents got separated in 1964 when he was two years old, and his father later died in a car accident in 1982. Barry was Barack's nickname when he was a kid.

Ann Dunham continued her studies and she was able to do so by leaving Barack in the care of Ann's parents, Barack's grandparents. While in the university, Ann usually spent her free time at the new East-West Center on campus. There she met an Indonesian named Lolo Soetoro and they dated and fell in love.

Barack and his mom
moved to Soetoro's rented
house in Upper Manoa
after Dunham and Soetoro
had a civil marriage
on March 15, 1965.

But after his step-dad graduated college in 1966, Soetoro went back to Indonesia. The following year, 1967, Barry's mom graduated and then they followed Soetoro to Indonesia. Barack was six years old when that happened.

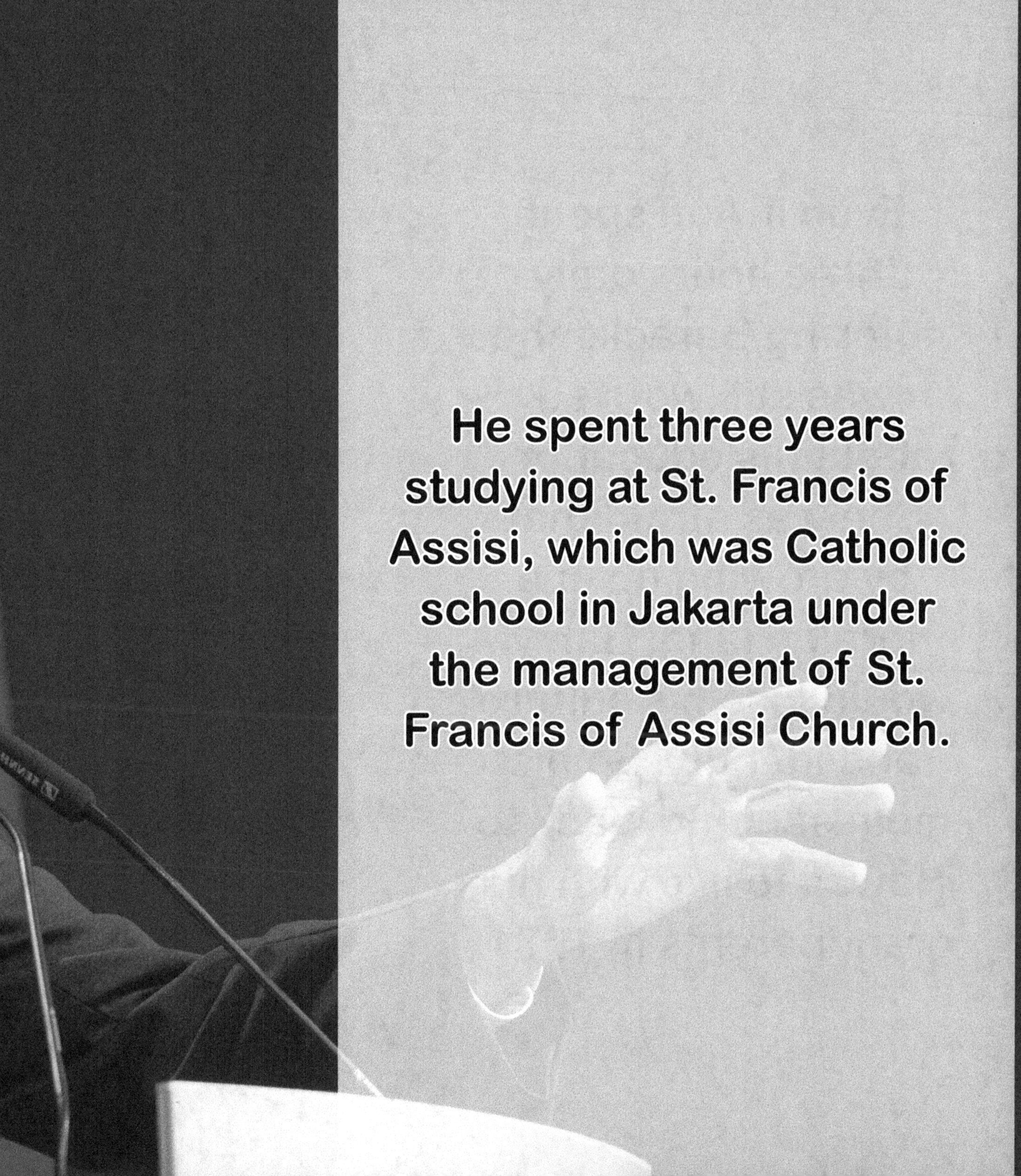
He spent three years studying at St. Francis of Assisi, which was Catholic school in Jakarta under the management of St. Francis of Assisi Church.

Even if Ann spent three hours daily tutoring Barack, she was still worried about his education. She was afraid that by growing up in a foreign land, Barry would lose his culture and identity. So his mom sent him back to Hawaii to live with his grandparents in 1971.

Barack spent those
few years in Jakarta,
Indonesia but mostly
spent his childhood
in the state of Hawaii
and was raised by
his grandparents.

The ten-year-old boy eagerly was welcomed by his grandparents and they enrolled him in one of the top private schools in Hawaii, known as Punahou School. Actress Kelly Preston and AOL founder Steve Case were his schoolmates.

Several months later,
his father surprised
him with a visit.
They went to a jazz
concert featuring
David Brubeck,
a legendary jazz
pianist. This was his
first and only chance
to meet his father
because his father
died in a car accident
eleven years later.

The following year, his mom and half-sister Maya went back to Hawaii. His mom got a scholarship from the University of Hawaii to pursue a master's degree in Anthropology. After she graduated three years later, Ann wanted to bring Barack back to Indonesia. However, Barack decided to stay in Hawaii. Two years, later Ann went back to finish her Ph.D and asked Barack to go with her to Indonesia. But still Barack declined.

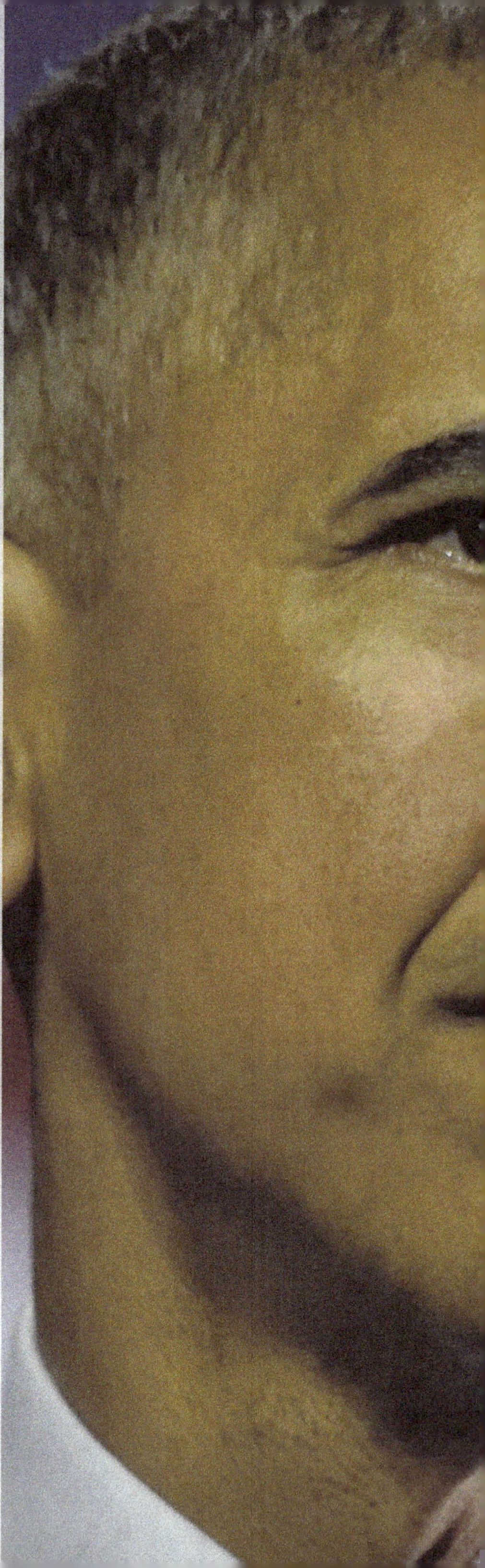

In high school, Barack was a respected and well-liked student. In the school's basketball team, he played as a forward and their team won the state championship in 1979. He was a very skillful basketball player that he was even called O'Bomber in high school.

Aside from his talent at basketball, he had a good voice and was a member of the Choir Club. He was also so good at writing that he became an editor of their school paper.

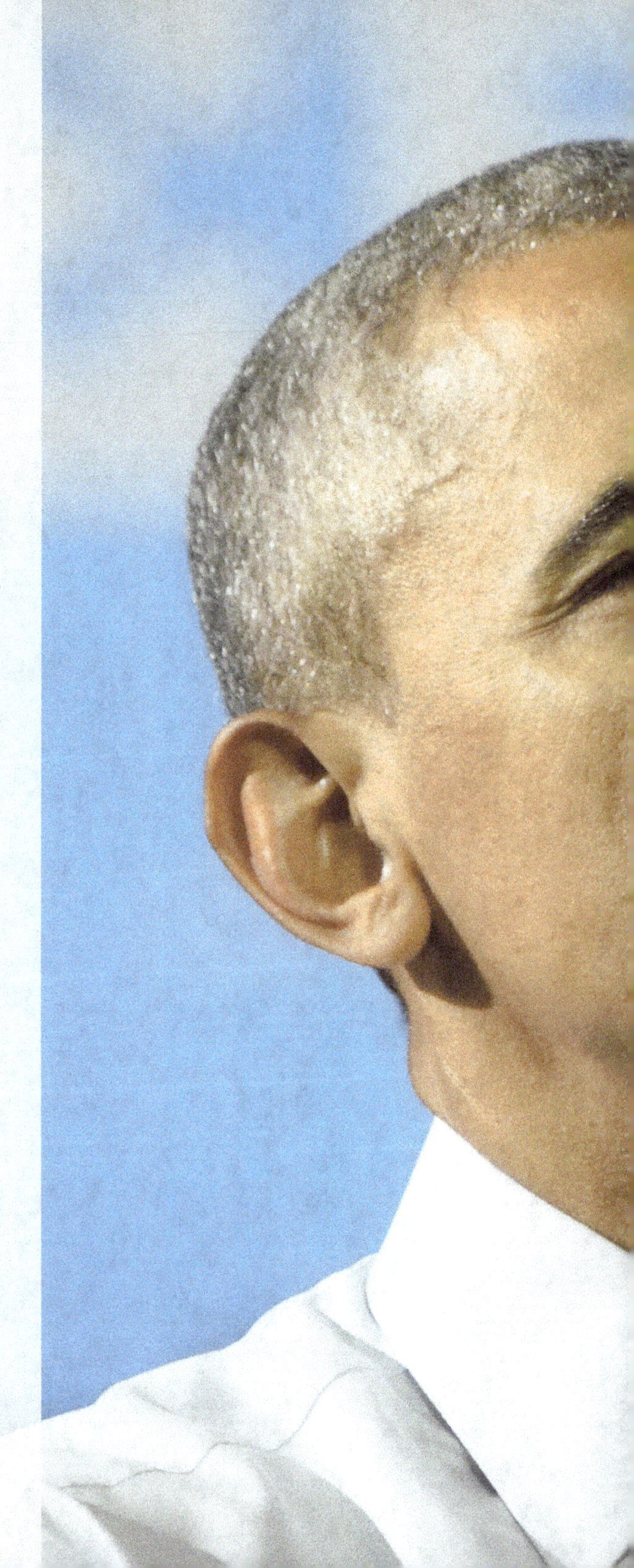

He also had a very colorful life outside of the school. He loves fishing, likes jazz music, and he was an avid surfer. He was really talented. He graduated high school in 1979.

Looking into his life, one can say that his excellence in academic performance, sports, and other areas of his life prepared him to become a great leader.

Visit
BABY PROFESSOR
EDUCATION KIDS
www.BabyProfessorBooks.com
to download Free Baby Professor eBooks
and view our catalog of new and exciting
Children's Books

www.ingramcontent.com/pod-product-compliance
Lightning Source LLC
Chambersburg PA
CBHW060145120726

48003CB00009B/3030